Deinonychus   *Ceratosaurus*   *Velociraptor*   skull

Diplodocus   *Giganotosaurus*   *Ankylosaurus*   duck

Eoraptor   palm tree   *Brachiosaurus*   *Allosaurus*

Apatosaurus   *Tyrannosaurus rex*   ferns   banana

explosion   fossil   skeleton   *Stegosaurus*   nest

Megalosaurus   *Maiasaura*   volcano   egg

Iguanodon   *Triceratops*   *Plateosaurus*   leaf

   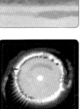  

 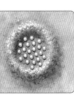

Dinosaurs

Written by Janine Amos
Reading consultants: Christopher Collier and Alan Howe,
Bath Spa University, UK

This edition published by Parragon in 2011
Parragon
Queen Street House
4 Queen Street
Bath BA1 1HE, UK

ISBN 978-1-4075-1828-2

Printed in China

Dinosaurs

PaRragon

Bath • New York • Singapore • Hong Kong • Cologne • Delhi
Melbourne • Amsterdam • Johannesburg • Auckland • Shenzhen

Parents' notes

This book is part of a series of non-fiction books designed to appeal to children learning to read.

Each book has been developed with the help of educational experts.

At the end of each book is a quiz to help your child remember the information and the meanings of some of the words and sentences. There is also a glossary of difficult words relating to the subject matter in the book, and an index.

Contents

6   What is a dinosaur?

8   Dinosaur world

10   Different dinosaurs

12   Dinosaur diets

14   *Stegosaurus*

16   Family life

18   *Triceratops*

20   Fierce or friendly?

22   *Tyrannosaurus rex*

24   Dinosaur death

26   Quiz

28   Glossary

30   Index

What is a dinosaur?

Dinosaurs were reptiles that walked on the Earth millions of years ago. Some dinosaurs were tiny, like birds. Others were giants – the largest land animals the world has ever seen.

Giganotosaurus (above) was the biggest dinosaur ever to have lived. Some of its teeth were longer than your hand.

Over thousands of years the bones, teeth, footprints and even poo of dead dinosaurs turned to rock. We call these fossils.

The first fossil of a dinosaur tooth ever discovered belonged to meat-eating *Megalosaurus* (below).

Today, dinosaur skeletons are displayed in museums.

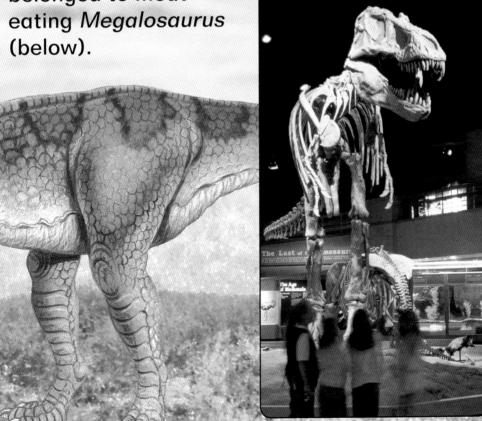

Dinosaur world

The Earth's history is split into lengths of time called periods. There were different kinds of weather, plants and animals in each period.

The **Triassic period** was hot. Palm trees, conifers and mosses grew on the Earth.

Eoraptor lived in the Triassic period.

Amazing!

The Triassic, Jurassic and Cretaceous periods belong to one length of time called the Mesozoic era. Dinosaurs ruled the land in the Mesozoic era.

In the wet **Jurassic period**, forests grew. *Diplodocus* and other large plant eaters had plenty to eat.

The **Cretaceous period** was cooler. Flowering plants grew, and there were more kinds of dinosaur than ever before.

Diplodocus lived in the Jurassic period.

Velociraptor lived in the Cretaceous period.

Different dinosaurs

Dinosaurs were large or small, heavy or light. Some had smooth bodies, others had spikes and horns. No one knows exactly how many kinds there were.

Velociraptor was a meat eater. It could run fast. Its short front legs were good for grabbing and holding prey.

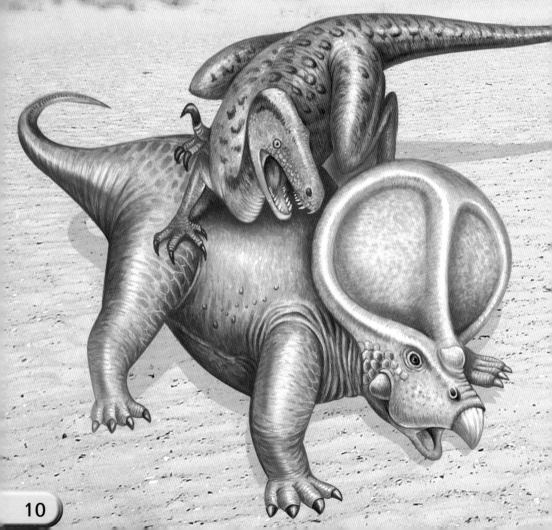

Ankylosaurus was covered with plates and spines. It was twice as wide as it was tall.

The plant-eating *Ankylosaurus* could defend itself against meat eaters with the bony club at the end of its tail.

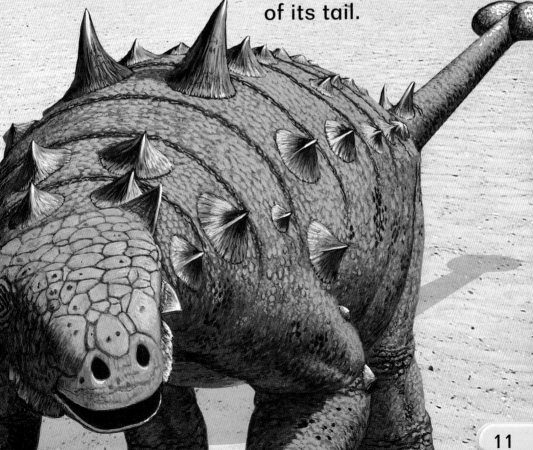

Dinosaur diets

Some dinosaurs ate the leaves of plants and trees. Other dinosaurs fed on any animal they could catch.

Allosaurus was a large meat eater. It had pointed teeth and powerful jaws.

Apatosaurus bones have been found with *Allosaurus* teeth marks on them.

Brachiosaurus was a plant eater. This dinosaur had a long neck, like a giraffe. It may have moved about in a herd, or group.

Ornithopod dinosaurs had beaks, like ducks. The beaks were perfect for chopping off plants and leaves.

Stegosaurus

Stegosaurus was a peaceful dinosaur – with a dangerous tail. Long spikes at the end gave it good protection.

Stegosaurus was hunted by meat eaters such as *Ceratosaurus* (right). If attacked, it hit out with its long, spiked tail.

Stegosaurus

Stegosaurus was a slow-moving plant eater. It lived in herds, feeding on leaves and ferns, such as these.

The bony plates on its back may have kept it cool, or they may have attracted other *Stegosaurus* dinosaurs.

The plates may have turned red when it was excited or afraid.

Family life

Dinosaur babies were born from eggs. Some mothers cared for their young. Others left the babies to look after themselves.

Maiasaura made a nest by scratching a hole in the ground.

The biggest dinosaur eggs were from *Hypselosaurus*. They were the size of a football.

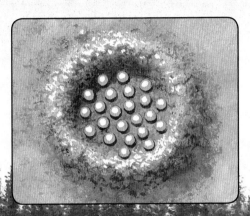

Maiasaura mothers laid about 25 eggs. They stayed near the eggs to protect them.

Maiasaura mothers covered their eggs with leaves to keep them warm.

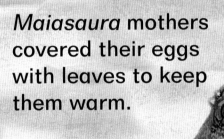

Triceratops

Triceratops was a horned dinosaur with a frill around its neck. It fed on plants. The frill was used to show off to other dinosaurs.

Triceratops would protect its babies. Its long, sharp horns could spear an enemy's flesh.

Triceratops was hunted by *Tyrannosaurus rex*. Marks made by *Tyrannosaurus* teeth have been found in *Triceratops* bones.

The name 'triceratops' means 'three-horned face'. *Triceratops* had a huge skull. Its neck frill was made of solid bone.

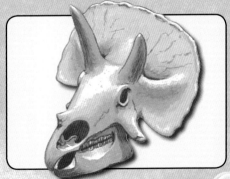

Fierce or friendly?

Some dinosaurs were peaceful plant eaters. Others were fierce hunters.

Like deer do today, *Iguanodon* fed on plants and leaves. These dinosaurs had big, spiked thumbs for holding down branches.

Small but fierce *Deinonychus* may have hunted in packs to bring down large animals.

Iguanodon lived in family groups.

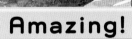

Amazing!

Iguanodon could bend its smallest finger across its hand to help it grab on to its food.

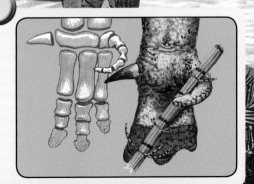

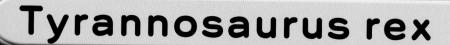

Tyrannosaurus rex

Tyrannosaurus rex was the king of the meat-eating dinosaurs. It had a huge head, with powerful, bone-crunching jaws.

Its mouth was filled with 50–60 pointed teeth. Some were as long as big bananas and they were very sharp.

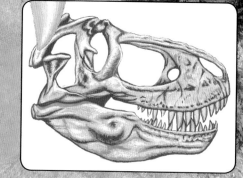

This dinosaur's arms were so tiny they didn't reach its mouth. But it could grab hold of its prey from behind.

Tyrannosaurus hid in the trees and then surprised its prey.

Dinosaur death

About 65 million years ago all the dinosaurs died out, or became extinct. Experts are not sure why.

Perhaps a huge rock fell from space and dust clouds blocked out the Sun. It may have become too cold for dinosaurs to live.

If a huge star exploded in space, deadly rays could have reached the Earth and killed the dinosaurs.

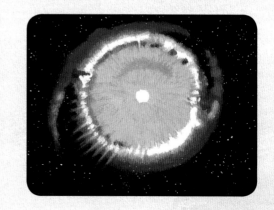

A lot of volcanoes were erupting 65 million years ago. Poisonous smoke could have killed the dinosaurs.

Amazing!

Thousands of rocks from space have been found on the Earth.

Quiz

Now try this quiz!
All the answers can be found in this book.

Which was the biggest dinosaur ever
to have lived?

(a) *Gigantosaurus*
(b) *Tyrannosaurus rex*
(c) *Diplodocus*

What did *Allosaurus* eat?

(a) Meat
(b) Plants
(c) Potato chips

How many teeth did *Tyrannosaurus rex* have?

(a) 10–20
(b) 50–60
(c) 150–160

How long ago did the dinosaurs die out?

(a) About 650 million years ago
(b) About 65 million years ago
(c) About 6 million years ago

Which dinosaur laid the biggest eggs?

(a) *Triceratops*
(b) *Maiasaura*
(c) *Hypselosaurus*

Which period of time did *Diplodocus* live in?

(a) The Triassic
(b) The Jurassic
(c) The Cretaceous

Glossary

Conifers   Trees and shrubs that have cones and thin leaves shaped like needles, but no flowers.

Cretaceous period   From 144 to 65 million years ago.

Extinct   When an animal or plant has died out completely so that there are none left anywhere on the Earth.

Fossil   A part or print of an animal or plant that has been turned to rock. Fossils can be millions of years old.

Jurassic period   From 206 to 144 million years ago.

Pack   A group of dinosaurs that hunts together.

Plate   A flat piece of bone on a dinosaur's body.

Prey   The animals that a dinosaur eats.

Reptile   An animal with dry, scaly skin. Most reptiles lay eggs with hard shells.

Skull   The bone in a dinosaur's head that protects its brain.

Triassic period   From 250 to 206 million years ago.

Index

a

Allosaurus 12
Ankylosaurus 11
Apatosaurus 12
arms and legs 10, 23

b

babies 16, 18
beaks 13
biggest dinosaur 6
bones 7, 12, 19
Brachiosaurus 13

c

Ceratosaurus 14
clubs 11
conifers 8
Cretaceous period 9

d

death of the dinosaurs 24,
    25
Deinonychus 21
Diplodocus 9

e

eggs 16, 17
Eoraptor 8
extinct 24

f

families 16-17, 21
ferns 15
forests 9
fossils 7
frills 18, 19

g

Giganotosaurus 6

h

herds 13, 15
horns 10, 18
hunting 20, 21
Hypselosaurus 17

i

Iguanodon 20, 21

j

jaws 12, 22
Jurassic period 9

m

Maiasaura 16, 17
meat-eating dinosaurs 7,
    10, 12, 14, 20, 22
Megalosaurus 7
Mesozoic era 9
mosses 8

mothers 16, 17
museums 7

n
necks 13
nests 16

o
ornithopod dinosaurs 13

p
packs 21
palm trees 8
periods 8, 9
plant-eating dinosaurs 9, 11, 12, 13, 15, 18, 20
plants 8, 9, 15
Plateosaurus 11
plates 11, 15
prey 10, 23

r
reptiles 6

s
skeletons 7
skulls 19
space rocks 24, 25
spikes 10, 14, 20
spines 11

stars, exploding 24
Stegosaurus 14-15

t
tails 11, 14
teeth 6, 7, 12, 19, 22
thumbs 20
Triassic period 8, 9
Triceratops 18-19
Tyrannosaurus rex 19, 22-23

v
Velociraptor 9, 10
volcanoes 25

Acknowledgements

Cover illustration: Jon Hughes and Russell Gooday

Illustrated by:
Norma Burgin, Mark Dobly, Graham Kennedy, Peter Konarnysky, Damain Quayle, Neil Reed, Pete Roberts (Allied Artists), James Field, Terry Riley (SGA), Mike Atkinson, Chris Forsey, Rob Shone, Q2A Media

Photography credits
t=top, c=centre, b=bottom, r=right, l=left

7tr Garry Gay/Getty, 7br Paul A. Souders/Corbis, 15tl Acerable/iStock, 17tr samkee/iStock